5 Ingredients Ketosis Diet Plans:

Burn Fat & Lose Weight In 4 Weeks Using These Ketosis Diet Plans That Requires 5 Ingredients Only

Ted Duncan

Table of Contents

Introduction.. **viii**

Chapter 1: Ketogenic Diet Basics **10**

The Ketosis Process... 11
Your Body as It Undergoes the Keto Transition12
Benefits of the Ketogenic Diet........................... 13
Risks of Undergoing the Keto Diet 14
Foods You Can Enjoy on the Ketogenic Diet.... 15
Foods You Can Eat on Occasion 18
Foods to Avoid on the Keto Diet 19

Chapter 2: Smoothies and Breakfast Recipes23

Overnight Apple Oatmeal 24
Sausage and Egg Casserole 26
Mixed Berry Cobbler Smoothie....................... 28
Butter Coffee 30
Eggs Benedict 32
Blackberry Almond Chia Pudding 34
Personalize Your Smoothie Bowl.....................36
Keto Morning Hot Pockets............................... 38
Keto Bagels 40
Breakfast Egg and Sausage Pie 42

Chapter 3: Soups and Salads **45**

Easy Broccoli and Cheese Soup 46
Roasted Tomato Soup 48
Low-Carb Cauliflower and Cheese Soup.......... 50
5-Minute Egg Drop Soup 52
Low-Carb Clam Chowder 54

King Keto Salad 56
Keto Mixed Green Spring Salad 58
Keto Potato Salad 60
Chickpea Egg Salad 62
Raw Kale Salad 64

Chapter 4: Side Dishes 67

Roasted Garlic and Lemon Cauliflower Rice ... 68
Cauliflower Mashed Potatoes 70
Keto Air Fried French Fries 72
Butternut Squash Noodles 74
Sweet Potato Latkes 76
Brussels Sprouts and Shallots with Balsamic
Glaze 78
Chipotle Sweet Potato Fries 80

Chapter 5: Snack Recipes 83

Broccoli Cheese Nuggets 84
Cheddar Parmesan Crisps 86
Bacon Wrapped Jalapeno Poppers 88
Coconut Butter Fat Bombs 90
Crunchy Kale Chips 92
Cheddar Taco Rolls 94
Avocado Egg-in-a-Hole Toast 96
Baked Tostones 98
Best Keto Guacamole 100

Chapter 6: Vegetable Recipes 103

Bean Sprout Stir-Fry 104
Roasted Spaghetti Squash 106
Roasted Parmesan Green Beans 108
Roasted Brussels Sprouts and Butternut Squash 110
Grilled Prosciutto Wrapped Asparagus 112

Shredded Brussels Sprouts with Lemon and Oil114
Maple Roasted Butternut Squash 116

Chapter 7: Fish and Seafood Recipes........ 119

Lemon and Dill Salmon 120
Spicy Shrimp 122
Parmesan Crusted Tilapia..........................124
Seared Mahi-Mahi......................................126
Cilantro Lime Shrimp 128
Maple Soy Glazed Salmon..........................130

Chapter 8: Poultry Recipes......................133

Salsa Chicken with Lime and Mozzarella 134
Green Chili Chicken 136
Chicken Tikka Masala 138
Chicken Salad Stuffed Avocado 140
Lemon Feta Chicken Drumsticks..................142
Easy Crock Pot Salsa Chicken Thighs.............144

Chapter 9: Pork Recipes 147

Bacon and Coleslaw Stir-Fry.........................148
Boneless Pork Chops 150
Low Carb Green Chili Pork Taco Bowl 152
Jamaican Pork Roast....................................154
Apricot and Rum Glazed Spiral Ham 156
Brown Sugar Ribs..158
Asian Citrus Pork Tenderloin 160

Chapter 10: Beef Recipes 163

Chipotle Steak Bowl 164
Reuben Casserole 166
Steak Tacos with Pork Rind Tortillas 168
Avocado Beef Bombs...................................170

Keto Beef Dip 172

Chapter 11: Sweet Recipes 175

Chocolate Peanut Butter Cups 176
Flourless Chocolate Cookies........................178
Dark Chocolate Nut Clusters...................... 180
Strawberry Cheesecake Fat Bombs 182
Coconut Crack Bars 184
Chocolate Chip Oatmeal Cookies 186
Crust-Less Cheesecake 188
Strawberries Romanoff 190
Pumpkin Purée 192

Chapter 12: Dressings and Sauces 195

Pickled Mayo Dressing 196
Raspberry Vinaigrette 198
Cranberry Pear Sauce 200
Keto Garlic Alfredo Sauce 202
Keto Buffalo Sauce....................................204

Chapter 13: My Favorite Ketogenic Ingredients 207

Conclusion.. 212

Introduction

I want to thank you for purchasing *5 Ingredients Ketosis Diet Plans: Burn Fat & Lose Weight In 4 Weeks Using These Ketosis Diet Plans That Requires 5 Ingredients Only.*

I am super excited you are here! It is no secret that the ketogenic diet is quickly becoming more than just a fad or a trend. It's now a go-to diet that many people have found success with when it comes to building muscle and shedding excess weight.

With the hustle and bustle of today's world, it has become increasingly harder for everyone to engage in a healthy lifestyle. After all, I am sure you know the satisfaction of picking up convenience food from your favorite fast food joint instead of taking the time to cook home-made meals after a long day. But with junk food, satisfaction comes at the expense of unhealthy habits. It also increases the chances of terrible health issues, and adds on to all that extra weight.

Time is valuable, which is why I've created this cookbook as a guide to healthier eating through many efficient ways. Each of the recipes mentioned in this book are made using only five ingredients or less! Yes, you read that right! And with fewer ingredients, you no longer have to worry about endless hours of shopping and can spend more time enjoying delicious meals.

If using five ingredients or less wasn't convenient enough, you will find that many recipes are made by using simple methods and easy-to-use kitchen appliances, from slow cookers to instant pots and beyond, you will be wondering where this cookbook has been all your life!

While there are many ketogenic diet cookbooks to choose from, this one is by far the most convenient for you and your busy lifestyle! Every effort was made to ensure it is full of as much useful information as possible, please enjoy!

If you enjoy the following content, click below to subscribe where we will notify you once we have a new book out!

Subscribers will always have discounts & priority access to new launches. You can even get to win exciting prizes & free books!

Click here -> http://bit.ly/nonfiction-subscribers-list

If you enjoyed the content, please leave a good review!

If not, please let us know why you did not at bookgrowthpublishing@mail.com and we will fix the issue for you.

Chapter 1:
Ketogenic Diet Basics

If you are reading this cookbook, then you probably know what the ketogenic diet is all about. But, for your sake and for those people who are just discovering what the ketogenic diet has to offer, this chapter will touch on the main basics that everyone should know to successfully get started on the keto diet.

The ketogenic diet primarily focuses on the increased consumption of fat and decreased consumption of carbohydrates. When consuming food that is high in carbs, your body naturally produces glucose and insulin.

- **Insulin** is a substance in the body responsible for processing glucose found in the bloodstream.

- **Glucose** is a substance our bodies need to convert and use carbohydrates, which is our body's primary energy source.

Since glucose is the energy source that our bodies have been conditioned to prefer, the fat we eat is stored and therefore, unused. Most of us consume carbs as our main source of energy, which is accurate according to what we have been taught. But what if I told you there was another way for you to shed off those excess pounds fast?

The Ketosis Process

The ketogenic diet is named and centered around the process of ketosis. This process involves a kind of metabolic state that our body goes into when we reduce our intake of carbohydrates. During ketosis, the body starts to use and burn fats as its primary source of energy. It also processes ketones that are found in the liver as well, which is a much better source of energy for our brains to utilize.

The ultimate goal of ketosis is to force your body into staying in this metabolic state. You are doing this by switching its fuel source. Thankfully, the human body is extremely adaptable, which means it can eventually switch to burning off ketones instead of using carbs. When you are burning those ketones at optimum levels, you will not only feel better and perform better both mentally and physically, but you can also lose weight at a much faster rate.

The core of the ketogenic diet is to drastically reduce carb intake with a high fat intake. It is similar to other low-carb diets but different in the fact that you are replacing carbohydrate-rich foods with foods that have a higher fat content. This tricks your body into metabolizing fats to produce energy, allowing it to get into better shape.

Your Body as It Undergoes the Keto Transition

By switching the fuel that your body needs to thrive, it is no secret that you will feel a bit different as you undergo this transition. Since the body is used to breaking down carbohydrates for energy, it has built up the necessary enzymes to process those carbs, which means it is not used to dealing with the processing and storage of fat as energy.

In other words, your body is going to deal with a lack of glucose, which means it needs to be given the time to create new enzymes to break down fats. When you physically get used to ketosis, your body naturally shifts to use the leftover glucose in your body. When you first start the keto diet, you could feel lethargic and lack energy, but no worries, this will not last too long.

The lethargy you will experience during the first week of the ketogenic diet is because of lack of electrolytes since most of it is being flushed from your system. This is why it is vital you drink plenty of water and fluids during this transition so that you can keep up with proper sodium intake levels. In fact, you should also be consuming a good amount of salt as well, since it helps to retain more water and replenishes those electrolytes.

Benefits of the Ketogenic Diet

Many diets that are based on a lower carbohydrate intake have been controversial since it is known that diets which are high in fats have the potential to raise cholesterol levels, resulting in heart diseases and other ailments. Among other diets, however, ones with lower carb intake wins the race in many aspects. They help with weight loss and are known for other benefits, such as lowering the risk for diseases and much more including:

- Increasing your body's ability to use fats as a fuel source
- Ketosis helps to utilize ketones
- Lowering insulin levels
- Suppressing hunger
- Helping expedite weight loss
- Reducing triglycerides
- Increasing good levels of cholesterol
- Reducing blood sugars
- Reducing blood pressure
- Natural treatment for cancer
- Effective in treating metabolic syndrome
- Natural remedy for many brain disorders

Risks of Undergoing the Keto Diet

While the benefits outweigh the risks, it is good to know what negative side effects that you will be facing while transitioning to a ketogenic lifestyle. I will say that many of these risks are not long-term ones and only happen during the beginning stages of the ketogenic diet.

- Muscle loss
- Development of ketoacidosis
- Deficiencies in micronutrients
- Change in lipids
- Brain god
- Fatigue
- Irritability

Foods You Can Enjoy on the Ketogenic Diet

- Grass-fed and wild animal sources:
  - Beef
  - Eggs
  - Fish and seafood
  - Gelatin
  - Ghee
  - Goat
  - Lamb
  - Liver, heart, kidneys, and other organ meats
  - Pork
  - Poultry
  - Venison
- Healthy fats:
  - Saturated
    - Butter
    - Chicken fat
    - Coconut oil
    - Duck fat
    - Ghee
    - Goose fat

- Lard
- Tallow
  - Monounsaturated
    - Avocado oil
    - Macadamia oil
    - Olive oil
  - Polyunsaturated
    - Fatty fish and seafood
- Non-starchy veggies
  - Leafy greens
    - Bok choy
    - Chard
    - Chives
    - Endive
    - Lettuce
    - Radicchio
    - Spinach
    - Swiss chard
  - Cruciferous vegetables
    - Dark leaf kale
    - Kohlrabi
    - Radishes
  - Asparagus
  - Bamboo shoots

- o Celery
- o Cucumber
- o Summer squash (spaghetti squash, zucchini)
- Fruits:
  - o Avocado
- Beverages and Condiments:
  - o Black coffee
  - o Bone broth
  - o Lemon/lime juice & zest
  - o Mayo
  - o Mustard
  - o Pesto
  - o Pickles and other fermented eats
  - o Pork rinds
  - o Spices
  - o Tea
  - o Water
  - o Whey protein

Foods You Can Eat on Occasion

- Vegetables and fruits:
  - Artichokes
  - Berries (mulberries, cranberries, raspberries, strawberries, blueberries, blackberries, etc.
  - Broccoli
  - Brussels sprouts
  - Cabbage
  - Cauliflower
  - Fennel
  - Root veggies (pumpkin, winter squash, mushrooms, etc.)
  - Sea vegetables
  - Sugar snap peas
  - Water chestnuts
- Full-fat dairy
- Nuts and seeds:
  - Macadamia nuts
  - Pecans, almonds, walnuts, hazelnuts, etc.
  - Sunflower seeds

Foods to Avoid on the Keto Diet

- Grains
    - Rice, corn, oats, wheat, barley, etc.
    - Pasta, bread, cookies, crackers, etc.
- Alcoholic and sweet beverages
- Artificial sweeteners
- Factory-farmed fish and pork
- Foods that are 'low-fat,' 'low-carb,' or 'zero-carb'
- Milk
- Processed foods
- Refined fats and oils
- Tropical fruits and fruit juices
- Soy products

Understanding Fats

While fats generally have garnered a bad rep over the years, we will be discussing both good fats and bad fats in the keto diet.

Good Fats

- Monounsaturated fats (MUFAs)
    - Avocados and avocado oil
    - Extra virgin olive oil
    - Goose fat
    - Lard and bacon fat
    - Macadamia nut oil
- Polyunsaturated fats (PUFAs)
    - Avocado oil
    - Chia seeds
    - Extra virgin olive oil
    - Fatty fish and fish oil
    - Flaxseeds and flaxseed oil
    - Nut oils
    - Sesame oil
    - Walnuts
- Saturated fats
- Butter
- Cocoa butter
- Coconut oil

- Cream
- Eggs
- Lard
- Palm oil
- Red meat
- Natural Trans Fats
  - Dairy fats such as butter and yogurt
  - Grass-fed animal products

Bad Fats

Processed and artificial fats are something you need to watch out for and avoid. From causing health issues to increased risks of cancer and diseases, remember to always have good fats by your side and limit or erase the consumption of bad fats.

Fats to eliminate:

- Hydrogenated and partially hydrogenated oils that are in processed products like cookies, crackers, margarine, and fast food

- Processed vegetable oils like cottonseed, sunflower, safflower, soybean, and canola oils

Chapter 2:
Smoothies and Breakfast Recipes

Overnight Apple Oatmeal

Calories 189 – *Fat* 5g – *Carbs* 1g – *Sugar* 6g – *Protein* 4g

Servings: 4

Ingredients:

- ¼ cup chopped pecans
- ¼ tsp. pumpkin pie spice
- 1 ½ cup water
- 1 cup chunky applesauce
- ¾ cup steel cut oats

Directions:

1. Add all of the ingredients in your crock pot and combine well.

2. Cover and set to cook for 8 hours on low setting.

Sausage and Egg Casserole

Calories 311 – Fat 12g – Carbs 2g – Sugar 0g – Protein 19g

Servings: 4-6

Ingredients:

- 8-ounces of shredded cheddar cheese
- 1-pound breakfast sausage
- 8 eggs

Directions:

1. Grease your crock pot with cooking spray.

2. In a pan, fry the sausage.

3. Beat eggs. Add half of the cheese and season with pepper and salt.

4. Pour the egg mixture into your crock-pot and sprinkle with cooked sausage. Top with remaining cheese.

5. Cover and cook for 5 to 6 hours on low.

Mixed Berry Cobbler Smoothie

***Calories** 97 – **Fat** 4g – **Carbs** 0g – **Sugar** 1g – **Protein** 2g*

Servings: *1*

Ingredients:

- 2-3 Medjool dates
- ½ cup blackberries
- ½ cup strawberries
- ½ cup blueberries
- ½ coconut milk

Directions:

1. Put all of the ingredients in a blender.

2. Blend mixture on high until you reach your desired texture.

3. Once smooth, add to a glass and enjoy!

Butter Coffee

Calories 230 – Fat 25g – Carbs 0g – Sugar 0g – Protein 0g

Servings: 1

Ingredients:

- 1 tbsp. coconut oil
- 1 tbsp. grass fed butter
- 2 tbsp. coffee
- 1 cup water

Directions:

1. Make a cup of coffee in whatever style or desire that suits you.

2. In a blender, mix together brewed coffee, butter and coconut oil. Blend for about 10 seconds. It should be creamy and light in color.

3. Pour into your favorite coffee mug and enjoy! Feel free to add other ingredients like whipped cream or cinnamon.

Eggs Benedict

Calories 297 – Fat 19g – Carbs 2g – Sugar 0g – Protein 30g

Servings: 4

Ingredients:

- 1 tsp. chives
- 1 tbsp. white vinegar
- 4 slices of Canadian bacon
- 4 eggs
- 4 Oopsie rolls

Directions:

1. Separate 2 eggs and whisk together yolks until they double in volume. Add a bit of lemon juice.

2. Boil about 3 ounces of water, reduce and bring it to a simmer, add salt and 1 tbsp. of white vinegar.

3. With a wooden spoon, make a whirlpool in the water by stirring a few times in one direction.

4. Crack an egg into a cup and lower into the whirlpool gently. Don't drop the egg in, lower the cup and let it out.

5. Cook egg for about 2-4 minutes, you want a runny consistency.

6. Lift egg out with a spatula and let it rest on a plate lined with paper towels.

7. Repeat with remaining eggs.

8. Fry Canadian bacon however you like.

9. Top oopsie rolls with bacon and place poached eggs on each slice of bacon.

Blackberry Almond Chia Pudding

Calories 109 – *Fat* 8g – *Carbs* 1g – *Sugar* 4g –
Protein 2g

Servings: 2-4

Ingredients:

- 2-3 tbsp. sliced almonds
- Drizzle of honey
- ¼ cup chia seeds
- 1 ½ cup vanilla almond milk
- 6-ounces fresh blackberries

Directions

1. Put blackberries in a bowl and crush with a fork until puréed.

2. Add honey, chia seeds, and milk to blackberry purée. Combine well and chill in the fridge overnight.

3. When serving, top with almonds and a few whole blackberries.

Personalize Your Smoothie Bowl

Calories 570 – Fat 35g – Carbs 2g – Sugar 2g – Protein 21g

Servings: 1

Ingredients:

- 1 scoop of low-carb protein powder
- 1 tbsp. coconut oil
- 2 tbsp. heavy cream
- ½ cup almond milk
- 1 cup spinach

Directions:

1. In a blender, mix together spinach, almond milk, cream, coconut oil, and ice. Blend until all ingredients are combined and have an even consistency.

2. Pour blended mixture into your bowl of choice.

3. Arrange toppings or throw them in and mix it all together.

Keto Morning Hot Pockets

Calories 287 – Fat 25g – Carbs 2g – Sugar 1g – Protein 24g

Servings: 2-4

Ingredients:

- 3 slices cooked bacon
- 2 tbsp. unsalted butter
- 2 eggs
- 1/3 cup almond flour
- ¾ cup mozzarella cheese

Directions:

1. Melt mozzarella cheese and mix with almond flour until combined.

2. Roll dough out between a couple of pieces of parchment paper.

3. Ensure your oven is preheated to 400 degrees.

4. Scramble your eggs in butter and place them within slices of bacon in the center of the dough.

5. Fold over the dough to seal.

6. Bake for 20 minutes until golden in color and firm when touched.

Keto Bagels

Calories 374 – *Fat* 31g – *Carbs* 8g – *Sugar* 1g – *Protein* 19g

Servings: 6

Ingredients:

- 1 tsp. baking powder
- 2 beaten eggs
- 3-ounces cream cheese
- 1 ½ cup almond flour
- 2 ½ cup shredded mozzarella cheese

Directions:

1. Mix baking powder, almond flour, cream cheese, and mozzarella cheese together.

2. Melt in microwave for 60 seconds, stir it well to combine.

3. Allow mixture to cool a bit before adding eggs.

4. Divide dough into 6 parts. With your hands, shape each portion into a round bagel.

5. Sprinkle each bagel with bagel seasoning mix or a pinch of sea salt if desired.

6. Ensure oven is preheated to 400 degrees. Bake bagels for 12 to 15 minutes until they start to turn gold at the edges.

Breakfast Egg and Sausage Pie

Calories 300 – Fat 23g – Carbs 1g – Sugar 0g – Protein 18g

Servings: 8

Ingredients:

- 1 cup shredded cheese of choice
- 1 tsp. garlic salt
- 10 eggs
- 2 tbsp. coconut flour
- 1-pound of sausage

Directions:

1. Ensure your oven is preheated to 350 degrees.

2. Grease a deep-dish pie plate.

3. Mix coconut flour and sausage together in the pie plate. Press mixture along the bottom of pie plate.

4. Crack your eggs into the plate over the sausage. Sprinkle eggs with garlic salt.

5. Bake for 45 minutes. Sprinkle with shredded cheese and then bake for another 15 minutes until cheese has melted and the eggs have completely set.

Chapter 3:
Soups and Salads

Easy Broccoli and Cheese Soup

Calories 291 – Fat 25g – Carbs 5g – Sugar 1g – Protein 13g

Servings: 8

Ingredients:

- 3 cup cheddar cheese
- 1 cup heavy cream
- 3 ½ cup chicken or bone broth
- 4 minced garlic cloves
- 4 cup broccoli florets

Directions:

1. Sauté garlic over medium heat until fragrant.

2. Add broccoli, heavy cream, and broth to pit. Increase heat until it begins to boil. Decrease heat and allow it to simmer for 10 to 20 minutes until broccoli becomes tender.

3. Add cheese and constantly stir until melted. Keep on a low simmer to avoid burning.

4. Remove from heat once the cheese is melted and enjoy!

Roasted Tomato Soup

Calories 95 – *Fat* 6g – *Carbs* 9g – *Sugar* 5g – *Protein* 2g

Servings: 6

Ingredients:

- ¼ cup heavy cream
- ¼ cup water
- 4 minced garlic cloves
- 1 tbsp. olive oil
- 10 Roma tomatoes

Directions:

1. Ensure your oven is preheated to 400 degrees. With foil, line a baking tray and with cooking spray, grease foil.

2. Toss chunks of Roma tomato in olive oil and garlic. Arrange on tray. Roast for 20 to 25 minutes until the tomato skins begin to pucker.

3. Place roasted tomato chunks into a blender and purée until smooth.

4. Pour tomato purée into a pot along with water. Season with pepper and salt.

5. Simmer for 10 to 15 minutes.

6. Mix in heavy cream.

Low-Carb Cauliflower and Cheese Soup

Calories 297 – *Fat* 11g – *Carbs* 12g – *Sugar* 4g – *Protein* 10g

Servings: 4

Ingredients:

- 1 cup cream cheese
- 4 cup chicken stock
- 5 cup cauliflower
- 1 crushed garlic clove
- 1 tbsp. extra virgin olive oil

Directions:

1. Warm up olive oil and add garlic. Cook for 1 to 2 minutes until fragrant.

2. Add cauliflower, cream cheese, and chicken stock. Season with pepper and salt.

3. Bring mixture to boil, decrease heat and let it simmer for 20 minutes until cauliflower becomes tender.

4. Blend mixture with an immersion blender or pour it into a regular blender.

5. Serve with a good grind of pepper and basil. If you wish, drizzle a bit of extra virgin olive oil over soup for a nice touch. Enjoy!

5-Minute Egg Drop Soup

Calories 289 – *Fat* 23g – *Carbs* 3g – *Sugar* 0g – *Protein* 15g

Servings: 1

Ingredients:

- 1 tsp. chili garlic paste
- 2 eggs
- 1 tbsp. bacon fat
- ½ cube chicken bouillon
- 1 ½ cup chicken broth

Directions:

1. Add bacon fat, bouillon cube, and chicken broth to a pot over medium heat.

2. Heat mixture until it boils, stir it well. Add chili garlic paste, stirring once more. Then turn off heat.

3. Beat eggs in another bowl. Pour eggs over broth.

4. Stir well and allow it to sit for a minute or so until cooked.

Low-Carb Clam Chowder

Calories 228 – Fat 16g – Carbs 11g – Sugar 4g – Protein 12g

Servings: 6

Ingredients:

- 1 cup heavy cream
- 1 ½ cup chicken broth
- 1 ½ cup unsweetened almond milk
- 1-pound cauliflower florets
- 2 6 ½-ounce cans of clams in juice

Directions:

1. In a pot, mix all the ingredients minus heavy cream together well. Bring mixture to a boil.

2. Decrease heat and allow it to simmer for 10 to 15 minutes until cauliflower becomes tender.

3. Mix in heavy cream, heating soup just enough to become hot again.

King Keto Salad

Calories 581 – Fat 43g – Carbs 9g – Sugar 2g – Protein 38g

Servings: 2

Ingredients:

- 4 tbsp. keto ranch dressing
- 4 cup mixed leafy greens of your choice
- 1 sliced avocado
- 6 thinly cut slices of bacon
- 2 boneless, chicken breasts

Directions:

1. Ensure your oven is preheated to 400 degrees.
2. Season chicken breasts with pepper and salt.
3. With ghee, grease a skillet and add breasts, skin side down.
4. Cook for 5 to 6 minutes until golden and crisp. Then, flip chicken and cook for another 30 seconds.
5. Place skillet in the oven. Cook for 10 to 15 minutes. Use a meat thermometer to measure the temperature, the chicken should be 165 degrees Fahrenheit.
6. With parchment paper, line a baking sheet and add bacon slices. Bake for 10 minutes until crispy.
7. Slice avocado and chicken.

8. To assemble the salad, place leafy greens into a serving bowl, then avocado, bacon, and chicken.
9. Top with a couple tablespoons of keto ranch dressing and devour!

Keto Mixed Green Spring Salad

Calories 393 – *Fat* 36g – *Carbs* 6g – *Sugar* 4g – *Protein* 14g

Servings: 1

Ingredients:

- 2 slices of bacon
- 2 tbsp. shave parmesan chees
- 2 tbsp. raspberry vinaigrette
- 3 tbsp. roasted pine nuts
- 2-ounces mixed greens

Directions:

1. Cook bacon until it is crispy.

2. Set greens aside in a container that can be easily shaken.

3. Crumble up cooked bacon and add to greens.

4. Toss remaining ingredients into greens. Shake the container well to distribute vinaigrette evenly throughout the salad.

Keto Potato Salad

Calories *224 –* ***Fat*** *17g –* ***Carbs*** *10g –* ***Sugar*** *3g – **Protein** 9g*

Servings: *4*

Ingredients:

- ¼ cup chopped green onion
- ½ cup chopped parsley
- 3 chopped pickles
- 6 hardboiled eggs
- 1 head of cauliflower, chopped into bite-sized pieces

Directions:

1. Chop up the head of the cauliflower into tiny florets. Steam for 2 to 3 minutes. Drain and set to the side to cool.

2. Peel the eggs and take out the yolks. Slice whites into small pieces and mix with the steamed cauliflower.

3. Combine the egg and cauliflower mixture with parsley, green onion, and pickle.

4. Toss mixture with mayo dressing.

5. Chill salad overnight.

Chickpea Egg Salad

Calories 375 – *Fat* 16g – *Carbs* 13g – *Sugar* 3g – *Protein* 20g

Servings: 4

Ingredients:

- 1 tbsp. chopped cilantro
- 2 tbsp. apple cider vinegar
- 2 tbsp. extra virgin olive oil
- 6 hardboiled eggs, sliced in half crosswise
- 2 15-ounce cans of chickpeas (rinsed and drained)

Directions:

1. In a bowl, toss all ingredients. Enjoy!
2. You can store it in the fridge for up to one week.

Raw Kale Salad

Calories 80 – *Fat* 6g – *Carbs* 3g – *Sugar* 1g – *Protein* 4g

Servings: 4

Ingredients:

- 1/3 cup grated parmesan cheese
- 1 tbsp. lemon juice
- ½ tsp. salt
- 1 tbsp. extra virgin olive oil
- 1 bunch of kale

Directions:

1. Remove ribs from the kale and slice into ¼-inch ribbons.

2. Mix kale with oil and salt. Massage kale for 3 minutes until it begins to soften.

3. Toss massaged kale with cheese and lemon juice.

Chapter 4:
Side Dishes

Roasted Garlic and Lemon Cauliflower Rice

Calories 124 – *Fat* 7g – *Carbs* 13g – *Sugar* 0g – *Protein* 5g

Servings: 2

Ingredients:

- 1 tsp. lemon juice
- 2 tsp. chopped parsley
- 3 chopped garlic cloves
- 1 tbsp. extra virgin olive oil
- 16-ounce riced cauliflower

Directions:

1. To rice cauliflower florets, chop them into small pieces and process in your food processor until the mixture resembles rice.

2. Ensure oven is preheated to 425 degrees Fahrenheit. With oil, grease a baking tray.

3. Combine riced cauliflower with garlic and olive oil, as well as a pinch of salt. Spread mixture out onto the prepared tray.

4. Bake for 25 minutes and make sure to turn it halfway through cooking. Rice will be slightly golden in color.

5. To serve, top with parsley and more lemon juice.

Cauliflower Mashed Potatoes

Calories 152– Fat 6g – Carbs 8g – Sugar 0g – Protein 3g

Servings: 2-4

Ingredients:

- Garlic powder
- 1 cup water
- 1 head cauliflower

Directions:

1. Core cauliflower and chop into chunks.

2. Place a trivet into the instant pot. Pour in water and add cauliflower to trivet.

3. Close lid.

4. Cook on 'MANUAL' for 3-5 minutes.

5. Perform a quick release.

6. Take out the cauliflower and empty the inner pot.

7. With an immersion blender, purée until you reach the desired consistency.

Keto Air Fried French Fries

Calories 176 – *Fat* 5g – *Carbs* 14g – *Sugar* 1g – *Protein* 4g

Servings: 1

Ingredients:

- 1/8 tsp. garlic powder
- 1/8 tsp. salt
- 1 tsp. extra virgin olive oil
- 1 Yukon gold or russet potato

Directions:

1. Ensure your air fryer is preheated to 380 degrees Fahrenheit. Liberally spray down air fryer basket with olive oil.

2. Cut potato into ¼-inch thin slices lengthwise. Then slice into ¼-inch fries.

3. Toss potatoes with oil and season with pepper, garlic powder, and salt.

4. Place coated fries into the basket.

5. Cook for 15 minutes, turning halfway. They will be crispy when done.

Butternut Squash Noodles

Calories 153 – Fat 5g – Carbs 19g – Sugar 0g – Protein 3g

Servings: 2

Ingredients:

- ¼ tsp. salt
- 2 tsp. extra virgin olive oil
- 20-ounces butternut squash

Directions:

1. Ensure your oven is preheated to 400 degrees Fahrenheit. Lightly spray two trays with oil.

2. Peel butternut squash and then proceed to cut off top portion.

3. Cut squash into 2 pieces. Spiralize squash into noodles.

4. Place spiralized squash onto baking trays. Drizzle with oil and season with pepper and salt.

5. Roast for 7 to 10 minutes until soft.

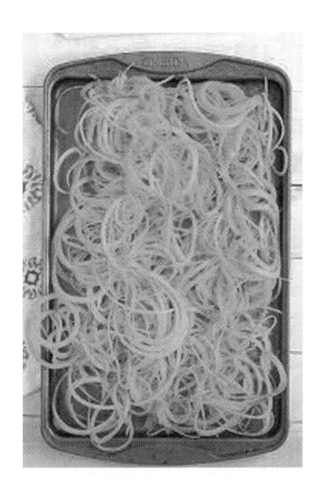

Sweet Potato Latkes

Calories 125 – Fat 7g – Carbs 11g – Sugar 4g – Protein 5g

Servings: 4

Ingredients:

- 4 tsp. extra virgin olive oil
- 4 crushed garlic cloves
- 2 beaten eggs
- ½ cup chopped scallions
- 1 peeled sweet potato

Directions:

1. Slice sweet potato in half. Spiralize potato.

2. Mix spiralized potato with garlic, eggs, and scallions, seasoning with pepper and salt.

3. In a skillet, heat up the oil.

4. Place a spoonful of seasoned potato into the skillet and spend 3 minutes cooking each side. Do this with all of the mixture. Press down as you are cooking potato mounds to create cake-like shapes.

Brussels Sprouts and Shallots with Balsamic Glaze

Calories 126– Fat 7g – Carbs 14g – Sugar 5g – Protein 4g

Servings: 4

Ingredients:

- 1 tbsp. balsamic glaze
- 2 shallots
- 1-pound of Brussels sprouts
- 2 tbsp. extra virgin olive oil

Directions:

1. Ensure your oven is preheated to 425 degrees.

2. Trim and slice shallots into ½-inch wedges. Trim and cut sprouts in half.

3. Heat olive oil in a good-sized pan. Add sprouts and shallots, let it cook for 3 minutes without stirring so it will caramelize.

4. Turn a few times for 2 to 3 minutes until veggies turn gold.

5. Place skillet in oven for 8 to 10 minutes to roast until veggies become softened. Drizzle with balsamic glaze and devour!

Chipotle Sweet Potato Fries

Calories 108– Fat 5g – Carbs 16g – Sugar 0g – Protein 1g

Servings: 2

Ingredients:

- Garlic powder
- Ground chipotle chili
- Sea salt
- 2 tsp. extra virgin olive oil
- 1 sweet potato

Directions:

1. Ensure your oven is preheated to 425 degrees.

2. Peel and cut sweet potato into ¼-inch fry-shaped pieces

3. Toss sweet potato fries with chili powder, garlic powder, salt, and olive oil.

4. Spread coated potato pieces onto the sheet.

5. Bake for 15 minutes. Turn and back for another 10 to 15 minutes until crispy.

Chapter 5:
Snack Recipes

Broccoli Cheese Nuggets

Calories 146 – *Fat* 9g – *Carbs* 5g – *Sugar* 1g – *Protein* 10g

Servings: 4

Ingredients:

- ¼ cup almond flour
- 1 cup shredded Monterey jack cheese
- 2 egg whites
- 2 cup cooked broccoli florets
- Pinch of salt

Directions:

1. Ensure your oven is preheated to 350 degrees. With parchment paper, line a baking tray.

2. Break up the broccoli into tiny pieces with a potato masher.

3. Add the other ingredients with mashed broccoli, mix it well.

4. Drop 20 scoops of the mixture onto your lined tray and form into nugget shapes.

5. Bake for 20 minutes until it becomes golden in color.

Cheddar Parmesan Crisps

Calories 152 – Fat 11g – Carbs 1g – Sugar 0g – Protein 11g

Servings: 4

Ingredients:

- 1 tsp. Italian seasoning
- ¾ cup shredded cheese of choice
- ¾ cup shredded parmesan cheese

Directions:

1. Ensure your oven is preheated to 400 degrees. With parchment paper, line a baking tray.

2. Stir the parmesan and shredded cheese of choice together.

3. Place the cheese mixture into similar sized heaps onto line tray, about 2-inches apart from one another.

4. Sprinkle each pile of cheese with Italian seasoning.

5. Bake for 6 to 8 minutes until edges begin to turn brown.

6. Let your cheese chips cool a bit before placing them on a paper towel to drain and get crispy. Snack away!

Bacon Wrapped Jalapeno Poppers

Calories 225 – *Fat* 18g – *Carbs* 3g – *Sugar* 1g – *Protein* 10g

Servings: 4

Ingredients:

- 1 tsp. paprika
- ¼ cup shredded cheddar cheese
- 4 ounces of cream cheese
- 16 strips bacon
- 16 fresh jalapenos

Directions:

1. Ensure that your oven is preheated to 350 degrees Fahrenheit.

2. Slice bacon in half so that you have 16 pieces cut into half-length.

3. Slice off ends of the jalapeños. Slice each pepper in half, length-wise, and ensure that you remove all seeds and innards.

4. Mix cheddar and cream cheese together.

5. Take the cheese mixture and proceed to fill each jalapeño half.

6. Engulf each jalapeño half with bacon.

7. Place jalapeño poppers on a foil-lined baking sheet. Ensure there is room between each popper.

8. Bake for 20-25 minutes.

Coconut Butter Fat Bombs

Calories 260 – *Fat* 26g – *Carbs* 0.5g – *Sugar* 2g – *Protein* 8g

Servings: 4

Ingredients:

- 1 pinch of salt
- 4 tsp. coconut butter
- 2 tbsp. erythritol
- 4 tbsp. coconut oil
- 4 tbsp. cocoa powder

Directions:

1. Mix together erythritol, cocoa powder, and coconut oil, keep stirring until there are no clumps left. Add a pinch of salt.

2. Pour about half the chocolate mixture evenly into four silicone cupcake molds. Tilt molds so that chocolate mixture coats edges. Freeze for around 5 minutes.

3. Spoon a tsp. of coconut butter into each mold. Tap the molds on a counter to ensure that the coconut butter spreads out evenly over chocolate later. Place in freezer again for a few more minutes.

4. Take remaining chocolate and cover the now hardened coconut butter. Freeze for five more minutes, and you are ready to enjoy!

Crunchy Kale Chips

Calories 180 – *Fat* 8g – *Carbs* 0.5g – *Sugar* 0g – *Protein* 4g

Servings: 2

Ingredients:

- 1 tsp. crushed red pepper
- 1 bunch of kale
- 1 tsp. garlic powder
- 2 tbsp. Parmesan cheese
- 2 tbsp. olive oil

Directions:

1. Ensure your oven is preheated to 350 degrees Fahrenheit.

2. Wash and thoroughly dry your bunch of kale.

3. Rip the kale into pieces, either leaving the stem on or by cutting it off.

4. Pour oil of your choice over kale and add the seasoning.

5. Toss kale and seasonings with hands to combine thoroughly. Almost every leaf should be shiny with oil.

6. On a cookie sheet, disperse kale leaves evenly.

7. Bake kale for 8 minutes. Check on them periodically. If chips are still soft, continue to bake at 2-minute intervals. Average baking time is 12 minutes.

8. When they're crunchy enough for your liking, take them out and put in a bowl.

Cheddar Taco Rolls

Calories 491– Fat 26g – Carbs 05g – Sugar 1g – Protein 19g

Servings: 2

Ingredients:

Crust:

- 2 cup shredded cheddar cheese

Topping:

- 2 tsp. Sriracha mayo or taco sauce
- ½ of an avocado, chopped
- ¼ cup chopped tomatoes
- 1 cup taco meat

Directions:

1. Ensure your oven is preheated to 400 degrees.
2. With parchment paper, line a baking sheet, ensuring that you leave room on the sides to line cheese up when it's done.
3. Grease parchment paper lightly, focusing especially on the edges.
4. Sprinkle shredded cheddar cheese to where the bottom of the pan is covered in a thin

layer. You may have to use more then 2 cups if necessary.

5. Stick it the in oven and bake for around 15 minutes until the cheese is bubbly and starts to turn brown in color.

6. Take the tray out of the oven.

7. Add taco meat, then bake for another 5-10 minutes until hot.

8. While baking, mix together the rest of the toppings in a small bowl until combined.

9. Remove sheet from oven, utilizing the sides of parchment, and pull off the cheese from the pan.

10. Add on cold toppings in a single layer.

11. Using a pizza cutter, cut top to bottom to make 3-4 slices.

12. Roll each slice from bottom to top.

Avocado Egg-in-a-Hole Toast

Calories 229– *Fat* 10g – *Carbs* 11g – *Sugar* 4g – *Protein* 12g

Servings: 1

Ingredients:

- 1 egg
- Olive oil
- 1-ounce of avocado
- 1 slice of whole grain bread

Directions:

1. With the rim of a glass, press a hole in the center of your whole grain bread slice.

2. With a fork, mash the avocado and season with pepper and salt.

3. Heat up an oil sprayed skillet and place the bread in it.

4. Crack the egg into the bread hole. Cook egg for 1 minute until the bottom sets, season with pepper and salt. Flip over and season the other side. Cook yolk to your liking.

5. Remove and top with avocado. I like my avocado toast with a dash or two of hot sauce!

Baked Tostones

Calories 137– Fat 1g – Carbs 19g – Sugar 11g – Protein 1g

Servings: 4

Ingredients:

- Salt
- 2 green plantains

Directions:

1. Ensure your oven is preheated to 425 degrees Fahrenheit. Grease a large baking tray.

2. Cut off the end of plantains. Score each on the two deepest sides so you can cut through the skin.

3. Place plantains in the microwave until they soften in the center.

4. Peel plantains and slice them into ¾-inch slices.

5. Smash hot plantains with the bottom of a glass to make them flat.

6. Place flattened plantains onto prepared tray. Season with salt.

7. Bake for 10 to 12 minutes until crispy and golden in color.

8. Season with additional salt if desired before crunching away!

Best Keto Guacamole

Calories 93– *Fat* 8g – *Carbs* 6g – *Sugar* 0g – *Protein* 1g

Servings: 8

Ingredients:

- 1 tbsp. chopped cilantro
- 1 mashed garlic clove
- 1/3 cup minced red onion
- 1 juiced lime
- 3 avocados

Directions:

1. Remove the pits from avocados and cut them in half. Remove the pulp from avocados and add to a bowl. Lightly mash avocado meat, leaving a few chunks.

2. Add remaining ingredients to mashed avocado, mix it well.

Chapter 6:
Vegetable Recipes

Bean Sprout Stir-Fry

Calories 98 – *Fat* 5g – *Carbs* 1g – *Sugar* 2g – *Protein* 6g

Servings: 2

Ingredients:

- 1 tsp. olive oil
- 2 tsp. soy sauce
- 2 garlic cloves
- 3 cup bean sprouts

Directions:

1. Warm up the olive oil and mince the garlic.

2. Add garlic to the now heated oil.

3. Rinse the bean sprouts.

4. When the garlic begin to turn brown, add the bean sprout, stir-fry them for about 2 to 3 minutes.

5. At the end of the cooking time, add soy sauce and fry for 60 more seconds. Enjoy!

Roasted Spaghetti Squash

Calories 42– *Fat* 1g – *Carbs* 10g – *Sugar* 4g – *Protein* 1g

Servings: 6

Ingredients:

- 1 large spaghetti squash
- Pepper and salt

Directions:

1. Preheat your oven to 350 degrees Fahrenheit.

2. Slice your squash in half. Scoop out seeds and fibers with the help of a spoon.

3. Place each half on baking sheets, season with pepper and salt.

4. Bake for 1 hour until you see the skin gives way under a little pressure, and the insides are tenderized.

5. Take out of the oven and let it cool for 10 minutes.

6. With a fork, scrape the inside of the squash to remove flesh.

7. Add flesh to a dish, season once more with a pinch of pepper and salt. Serve hot!

Roasted Parmesan Green Beans

Calories 55– Fat 3g – Carbs 6g – Sugar 0g – Protein 3g

Servings: 4

Ingredients:

- 1 ½ tbsp. shredded parmesan cheese
- ¼ tsp. garlic powder
- 2 tsp. extra virgin olive oil
- 12-ounces green beans

Directions:

1. Preheat your oven to 425 degrees Fahrenheit. With foil, line a baking tray.

2. Lay out your beans and top with oil. Season with pepper, salt, and garlic powder, toss it well to coat evenly.

3. Spread coated green beans onto the tray. Bake for 10 minutes, make sure to turn them halfway through cooking. Take it out of the oven and sprinkle with grated parmesan. Enjoy!

Roasted Brussels Sprouts and Butternut Squash

Calories 103 – Fat 5g – Carbs 9g – Sugar 3g – Protein 3g

Servings: 6

Ingredients:

- 6 sprigs of thyme
- 16-ounces butternut squash
- 16-ounces Brussels sprouts
- 2 tbsp. extra virgin olive oil

Directions:

1. Preheat your oven to
2. 425 degrees Fahrenheit. With oil, spray a large pan.
3. Peel and dice the butternut squash into ¾-inch pieces. Slice sprouts in half.
4. Toss squash and sprouts with oil and ¾ of a teaspoon of both pepper and salt.
5. Arrange veggies onto the tray.
6. Bake for 40 minutes until veggies are roasted and tenderized.

Grilled Prosciutto Wrapped Asparagus

Calories 50 – *Fat* 3g – *Carbs* 3g – *Sugar* 1g – *Protein* 4g

Servings: 4

Ingredients:

- 4 sliced of prosciutto
- 16 asparagus spears
- Extra virgin olive oil

Directions:

1. Slice the prosciutto into 4 pieces.

2. Snap off the ends of the asparagus spears.

3. Wrap each spear in a piece of prosciutto.

4. Sprinkle with olive oil and season with pepper and salt.

5. Grill over light heat for 5 to 6 minutes, make sure to turn it every few minutes.

Shredded Brussels Sprouts with Lemon and Oil

Calories *80–* ***Fat*** *7g –* ***Carbs*** *5g –* ***Sugar*** *1g –*
Protein *2g*

Servings: *4*

Ingredients:

- Juice of 1 lemon
- 2 tbsp. extra virgin olive oil
- 6-ounces Brussels sprouts

Directions:

1. Trim off the stem from the sprouts and slice lengthwise in half. Shred sprouts finely.

2. Place the shredded sprouts into a serving bowl and toss with lemon juice and olive oil. Season with salt and pepper.

Maple Roasted Butternut Squash

*Calories 104– **Fat** 2g – **Carbs** 18g – **Sugar** 7g – **Protein** 1g*

Servings: *4*

Ingredients:

- 2 ½ tbsp. pure maple syrup
- ½ tbsp. extra virgin olive oil
- 1 ¼-pounds butternut squash

Directions:

1. Preheat your oven to 400 degrees Fahrenheit.

2. Peel and dice butternut squash into ¾-inch pieces.

3. Toss squash chunks with pepper, salt, maple syrup and olive oil. Pour mixture into a baking dish and cover with foil.

4. Roast squash for 25 minutes.

5. Discard foil and bake squash for another 15 minutes until tender.

Chapter 7:
Fish and Seafood Recipes

Lemon and Dill Salmon

Calories 172 – *Fat* 10g – *Carbs* 1g – *Sugar* 0g – *Protein* 11g

Servings: 4

Ingredients:

- 2 finely chopped sprigs of dill
- Juice of 2 lemons
- 1-pound salmon fillet

Directions:

1. Cover the bottom of your slow cooker with parchment paper.

2. Cut fillets into four portions and place it in your slow cooker.

3. Sprinkle fillets with pepper and salt and drizzle with lemon juice. Place sprigs of dill over the salmon.

4. Set slow cooker to cook on high for 1 hour.

5. Lift salmon out of slow cooker and remove the skin before enjoying.

6. When serving, drizzle salmon with more lemon juice.

Spicy Shrimp

Calories 94 – *Fat* 5g – *Carbs* 1g – *Sugar* 0g – *Protein* 11g

Servings: 4

Ingredients:

- 1-2 shakes of cayenne pepper
- 1-2 shakes of chili powder
- 1-2 shakes of garlic salt
- 1-pound shrimp
- 1 tbsp. olive oil

Directions:

1. Heat oil.

2. Pat shrimp with paper towels until dry. Place in a pan and sprinkle with seasonings.

3. Cook for a few minutes and add a splash of broth so that spices come up from pan. This will be the sauce coating for shrimp.

4. Serve with mashed cauliflower and kale!

Parmesan Crusted Tilapia

Calories 204 – *Fat* 14g – *Carbs* 4g – *Sugar* 1g – *Protein* 26g

Servings: 4

Ingredients:

- 4 tilapia filets
- 1 tbsp. extra-virgin olive oil
- 1 tbsp. parsley
- 2 tsp. paprika
- ¾ cup grated parmesan

Directions:

1. Preheat your oven to 400 degrees. Line a baking tray with foil.

2. Mix a pinch of salt, parsley, paprika, and parmesan cheese together.

3. Drizzle tilapia in olive oil and dredge in cheese mixture. Place on the tray.

4. Bake for 10-12 minutes. Serve with lemon wedges.

Seared Mahi-Mahi

Calories 169– Fat 11g – Carbs 1g – Sugar 0.5g – Protein 19g

Servings: 2

Ingredients:

- 1 ½ tsp. Cajun seasoning
- ½ tsp. garlic
- 1 ½ tbsp. + 1 tsp. avocado oil
- 2 skinless Mahi Mahi fillets

Directions:

1. Coat both sides of fish with avocado oil and season with Cajun seasoning, garlic, pepper, and salt.

2. In a skillet over high heat, warm up 1-2 tbsp. of avocado oil. When it starts to shimmer, add fillets to pan. Cook for 5 minutes per side until mahi-mahi is opaque in color.

Cilantro Lime Shrimp

Calories 119– *Fat* 3g – *Carbs* 2g – *Sugar* 0g – *Protein* 19g

Servings: 6

Ingredients:

- 2 tbsp. lime juice
- 2 tsp. extra virgin olive oil
- ¼ tsp. + 1/8 tsp. cumin
- 1 ½-pounds deveined and peeled jumbo shrimp
- 5 crushed garlic cloves

Directions:

1. Season shrimp with pepper, salt, and cumin.

2. Warm up half of the olive oil in a skillet. Add half of the shrimp, allowing it to cook undisturbed for 2 minutes. Flip shrimp over and cook until opaque in color.

3. Add remaining olive oil and shrimp, repeating step 2.

4. Return all of the shrimp to the skillet and mix in garlic, making sure it's evenly mixed.

5. Squeeze lime juice on top of shrimp. Toss well and eat!

Maple Soy Glazed Salmon

Calories 293 – *Fat* 11g – *Carbs* 12g – *Sugar* 10g – *Protein* 35g

Servings: 4

Ingredients:

- 4 skinless wild salmon filets
- 1 smashed garlic clove
- 3 tbsp. soy sauce
- 3 tbsp. pure maple syrup
- 1 tbsp. Sriracha sauce

Directions:

1. Mix garlic, Sriracha, soy sauce, and maple syrup together and then pour into a resealable bag. Add salmon to bag and let marinate for 1 hour.

2. Ensure your oven is preheated to 425 degrees Fahrenheit. Grease a baking tray.

3. Take out fish from the marinade and pat dry. Add marinade mixture to a bowl.

4. Put fish on a tray and bake for 8 to 10 minutes.

5. Heat marinade mixture to a slow simmer and allow it to reduce and thicken.

6. Spoon glaze over the salmon and enjoy!

Chapter 8:
Poultry Recipes

Salsa Chicken with Lime and Mozzarella

Calories 327 – *Fat* 14g – *Carbs* 3g – *Sugar* 1g – *Protein* 12g

Servings: 2-3

Ingredients:

- 1 cup grated mozzarella cheese
- 2 tbsp. freshly squeezed lime juice
- 4 boneless, skinless chicken breasts
- 2 cup medium or mild salsa

Directions:

1. In a saucepan, add salsa and simmer over low heat until it's reduced to about one cup.

2. Trim fat from the chicken and cut each lengthwise in half.

3. Grease your slow cooker with a cooking spray and place the meat in a single layer inside the cooker. Season with pepper and salt.

4. Stir lime juice into reduced salsa and then pour salsa mixture over chicken. Set it to cook slowly for 60 to 90 minutes until the chicken is completely cooked.

5. Once cooked, ensure your broiler is preheated and grease a glass dish.

6. Remove chicken pieces with a slotted spoon and place in glass dish. Spoon salsa over chicken.

7. Sprinkle mozzarella cheese over chicken and broil for 5 minutes until slightly browned. Serve with sour cream!

Green Chili Chicken

Calories 290 – *Fat* 5g – *Carbs* 1g – *Sugar* 0.5g – *Protein* 23g

Servings: 8-10

Ingredients:

- 4-ounce can roasted green chilies
- 1 tsp. cumin
- 2 smashed garlic cloves
- 8-ounces green salsa
- 2 ½ - 3 pounds boneless, skinless chicken breast

Directions:

1. In your slow cooker, mix all ingredients except the chicken until combined.

2. Place chicken in green salsa and season with pepper and salt.

3. Set to cook on low for 6 to 8 hours.

4. If you desire a thicker sauce, cook for another 30 minutes on high until the sauce is reduced further.

5. Shred chicken with forks.

Chicken Tikka Masala

Calories 380 – *Fat* 6g – *Carbs* 5g – *Sugar* 5g – *Protein* 22g

Servings: 2

Ingredients:

- ¼ tsp. ginger
- 1 tbsp. lemon juice
- 1 tbsp. garam masala
- 1 cup 2% plain Greek yogurt
- 1-pound boneless skinless chicken breast

Directions:

1. Press 'SAUTE' on the instant pot. Add chunks of chicken and sauté for 5 minutes until it has cooked on all sides.

2. Set instant pot to 'HIGH.' Pour in all sauce components into the pot on top of chicken and combine well. Cover with lid. Push 'MANUAL' and let it cook for 10 minutes. Perform a quick release.

3. Push SAUTE again. Once the pot has warmed, add cream, combine them well. Allow the contents to simmer until it becomes as thick as you would like.

4. Serve on top of rice. Top with cilantro if
   desired. Enjoy!

Chicken Salad Stuffed Avocado

Calories 570 – *Fat* 45g – *Carbs* 5g – *Sugar* 3g – *Protein* 29g

Servings: 1

Ingredients:

- sour cream
- 1 medium avocado
- 1 stalk of celery
- 1 tbsp. diced red onion
- 3-ounces of cooked and shredded chicken breast

Directions:

1. Cook chicken breast on low heat until it's cooked thoroughly, then shred using two forks.

2. In a bowl, mix together the celery, red onion and chicken.

3. Cut and pit an avocado. Place some of the scooped out avocado into a bowl.

4. Add sour cream, salt, and pepper.

5. Toss all the ingredients together and spoon it back into avocado halves.

Lemon Feta Chicken Drumsticks

Calories 195– *Fat* 7g – *Carbs* 3g – *Sugar* 0.5g – *Protein* 28g

Servings: 4

Ingredients:

- 1/3 cup grated feta cheese
- Juice of 1 lemon
- 1 tbsp. dried oregano
- 2 tsp. garlic powder
- 8 skinless chicken drumsticks

Directions:

1. With pepper, salt, oregano, garlic powder, and lemon juice, season chicken.

2. Place seasoned chicken into your slow cooker.

3. Cook on high for 4 hours until the chicken is cooked thoroughly and is no longer pink.

4. Sprinkle with feta cheese and cover, wait for the cheese to melt.

Easy Crock Pot Salsa Chicken Thighs

Calories 187– Fat 8g – Carbs 3g – Sugar 0g – Protein 30g

Servings: 6

Ingredients:

- ¾ tsp. cumin
- ¼ tsp. garlic powder
- Adobo seasoning
- 1 cup chunky salsa
- 1 ½-pounds lean skinless chicken thigh fillets

Directions:

1. Season your chicken filets with adobo seasoning and add them to your crock pot along with ½ a teaspoon of cumin, garlic powder, and salsa.

2. Set the pot to cook for 4 hours on low.

3. Remove the chicken and shred with forks.

4. Pour cooking liquids into a bowl and add shredded chicken back to the crockpot.

5. Season with salt and remaining cumin.

6. Add ¾ of a cup of reserved cooking liquid back to the pot and cover until you are ready to eat.

Chapter 9:
Pork Recipes

Bacon and Coleslaw Stir-Fry

Calories 210 – *Fat* 11g – *Carbs* 4g – *Sugar* 4g – *Protein* 7g

Servings: 2

Ingredients:

- 1 bag of coleslaw mix
- 5-6 strips chopped bacon
- 1 chopped onion
- 3 chopped garlic cloves
- 1 tbsp. coconut oil

Directions:

1. Melt the coconut oil in a pan. Then add bacon, onion, and garlic. Cook the bacon until it reaches your desired level of crispiness.

2. Add coleslaw mix, stir until it is coated well with bacon fat. Stir-fry mixture for 10 minutes until the coleslaw becomes soft and slightly translucent.

Boneless Pork Chops

Calories 210 – *Fat* 11g – *Carbs* 4g – *Sugar* 4g – *Protein* 7g

Servings: 2

Ingredients:

- 1 cup water
- 1 package ranch mix
- 1 stick butter
- 4-6 boneless pork chops
- 1 tbsp. coconut oil

Directions:

1. Put the pork chops in an instant pot along with the coconut oil.

2. Push SAUTE and brown all sides.

3. Put butter on top of the chops and sprinkle with ranch mix.

4. Pour water over the pork chops.

5. Put on lid.

6. Push MANUAL and set it to cook for 5 minutes.

7. Allow pressure to release naturally.

8. Drizzle with buttery sauce on top of pork chops when serving.

Low Carb Green Chili Pork Taco Bowl

Calories 354 – *Fat* 14g – *Carbs* 4g – *Sugar* 2g – *Protein* 17g

Servings: 2

Ingredients:

- 16-ounces of green chili salsa
- 1 tbsp. olive oil
- 2 tsp. garlic powder
- 2 tsp. cumin
- 2 pounds pork sirloin

Directions:`

1. Trim pork and cut into slices against the grain.

2. Mix pepper, salt, garlic powder, and cumin together and then rub onto pork.

3. Press SAUTE on the instant pot and brown pork on all sides.

4. Pour in the green chili salsa.

5. Lock lid and push MANUAL to cook on HIGH for 45 minutes.

6. Serve with cauliflower rice.

Jamaican Pork Roast

Calories 354 – *Fat* 14g – *Carbs* 4g – *Sugar* 2g – *Protein* 17g

Servings: 2

Ingredients:

- Beef stock
- 1 tbsp. olive oil
- ¼ cup Jamaican Jerk spice blend
- 4 pounds pork shoulder

Directions:

1. Rub down roast with olive oil and spice blend.

2. Push SAUTE on instant pot. Brown the meat on all sides.

3. Pour in beef broth.

4. Seal with lid. Press MANUAL to cook on HIGH for 45 minutes.

5. Perform a quick release.

6. Shred pork and serve.

Apricot and Rum Glazed Spiral Ham

Calories 145– *Fat* 7g – *Carbs* 10g – *Sugar* 9g – *Protein* 15g

Servings: 8-10

Ingredients:

- 3 tbsp. dark rum
- 3 tbsp. apricot preserves
- 1 (6 to 8-pound) hickory smoked cooked spiral ham

Directions:

1. Preheat your oven to 325 degrees.

2. Place ham into a roasting pan along with a cup of water. Bake for an hour.

3. As the ham is being baked, make glaze by pouring rum and preserves in a pan, whisk it for 5 to 8 minutes until it starts to bubble.

4. Remove ham and brush with apricot and rum glaze. Then put in glazed ham back in and bake for another 50 to 60 minutes.

Brown Sugar Ribs

Calories 271 – *Fat* 10g – *Carbs* 2g – *Sugar* 7g – *Protein* 16g

Servings: 4

Ingredients:

- 1 sweet onion
- 1 ½ pounds boneless pork ribs
- 2 tbsp. seasoned rice vinegar
- ¼ cup brown sugar
- 1/3 cup soy sauce

Directions:

1. Whisk vinegar, brown sugar, and soy sauce together in your slow cooker.

2. Cut onion into quarters and cut into thin slices.

3. Add ribs and onions to the slow cooker, thoroughly coat the meat with sauce.

4. Set it to cook ribs for 4 hours on high for 6 to 8 hours on low setting.

5. Ensure that you flip your meat halfway through the cooking process.

Asian Citrus Pork Tenderloin

Calories 304 – Fat 5g – Carbs 2g – Sugar 4g – Protein 21g

Servings: 6-8

Ingredients:

- 1-inch grated ginger
- 1 minced garlic clove
- 2 tbsp. orange preserves
- 1/3 cup soy sauce
- 2-pounds of pork tenderloins

Directions:

1. Mix ginger, garlic, orange preserves, and soy sauce together.

2. Place tenderloins into your slow cooker and season with pepper and salt.

3. Pour sauce over the tenderloin.

4. Set cooker to cook for 1 to 2 hours on low until the center of tenderloin reaches 140 degrees Fahrenheit on the meat thermometer.

5. Preheat your broiler, set the rack 6 inches below it.

6. Place pork on a baking sheet lined with foil.

7. Place cooking sauce and juices in a small pan. Simmer for 5 minutes until it's reduced.

8. Spoon sauce over pork and broil for 5 minutes. Allow meat to rest for 5 minutes before attempting to cut.

9. When serving, sprinkle with chopped scallions and accompany with sauce.

Chapter 10:
Beef Recipes

Chipotle Steak Bowl

Calories 620 – Fat 31g – Carbs 6g – Sugar 4g – Protein 22g

Servings: 4

Ingredients:

- 1 handful of fresh cilantro
- 1 cup sour cream
- 4 ounces of pepper jack cheese
- 1 guacamole recipe
- 16 ounces of skirt steak

Directions:

1. In a warm cast iron skillet, season skirt steak with salt and pepper and cook each side up to 3-4 minutes on high heat. Let it rest while you prepare guacamole.

2. Slice steak against the grain into thin, bite-sized strips and divide it into four even portions.

3. Shred pepper jack cheese and top each portion of meat.

4. Add ¼ cup of guacamole to each portion, followed by a ¼ cup of sour cream.

Reuben Casserole

Calories 433 – *Fat* 27g – *Carbs* 12g – *Sugar* 9g – *Protein* 30g

Servings: 4

Ingredients:

- 8-ounces grated Swiss cheese
- 12-ounces deli sliced corned beef
- ½ cup Russian dressing
- 1 tomato
- 2-pound bag sauerkraut

Directions:

1. Preheat your oven to 350 degrees. Grease a baking dish.

2. Pour sauerkraut into the bottom of the dish.

3. Cut tomato into four evenly sliced rounds and layer over the sauerkraut.

4. Drizzle tomatoes with dressing and then add corned beef. Sprinkle with grated Swiss cheese.

5. Bake for 20 to 25 minutes until heated through.

Steak Tacos with Pork Rind Tortillas

Calories *356* – *Fat* *12g* – *Carbs* *4g* – *Sugar* *2g* – *Protein* *23g*

Servings: *2-3*

Ingredients:

- 2 6-ounce sirloin steaks
- 2 tbsp. cream cheese
- 1 egg
- ¾ cup mozzarella cheese
- 1 cup crushed pork rinds

Directions:

1. In a food processor, crumble pork rinds.

2. Melt cream cheese and mozzarella together in a microwave. Add crushed pork rinds to cheese mixture. Form into balls. Place dough in between parchment. Roll out dough to the thickness you desire. Cut out circles and place on a tray. Cook for 3-5 minutes per side until slightly browned.

3. For steak, allow the meat to sit on the side until it reaches room temperature. Season with steak seasoning of choice, pepper, and salt.

4. Heat up avocado oil and sear steak on each side until it has cooked well. Let the meat rest for at least 10 minutes before slicing.

5. Add meat to pork rind shells and garnish with toppings of choice.

Avocado Beef Bombs

Calories *249* – **Fat** *18g* – **Carbs** *1g* – **Sugar** *1g* – **Protein** *5g*

Servings: *12-14*

Ingredients:

- Sugar-free BBQ sauce
- Raw/thinly sliced bacon
- Cheese of choice
- 4 avocados
- 1 ½ pounds ground beef

Directions:

1. Cut avocados in half and take out pits. Peel skins off each half.

2. Cut choice of cheese into cubes and place into the centers of the avocados.

3. Split ground beef into 4 equal sized sections. Season with pepper and salt. Mold beef into sections around each avocado and cheese.

4. Layer with raw bacon until avocado is covered.

5. Grill for 30-40 minutes until the bacon and beef have completely cooked, and the cheese inside has melted. Feel free to brush on BBQ

sauce while cooking or use it on the meat after cooking.

Keto Beef Dip

Calories 146 – *Fat* 8g – *Carbs* 1g – *Sugar* 3g – *Protein* 2g

Servings: 8

Ingredients:

- 4 ounces diced beef
- 1 tsp. garlic powder
- 1 tbsp. Worcestershire sauce
- 8 ounces sour cream
- 8 ounces softened cream cheese

Directions:

1. Preheat oven to 350 degrees.

2. Mix sour cream and cream cheese together until smooth. Add Worcestershire sauce and garlic powder, mix them well.

3. Then mix in onions and beef until combined.

4. Bake for 20-30 minutes until bubbly and hot.

Chapter 11:
Sweet Recipes

Chocolate Peanut Butter Cups

Calories 214 – *Fat* 22g – *Carbs* 3g – *Sugar* 0.5g – *Protein* 2g

Servings: 12

Ingredients:

- ¼ cup natural peanut butter
- ¼ cup heavy cream
- 4 packets sweetener of choice
- 2-ounces unsweetened chocolate
- 1 cup butter

Directions:

1. Using a microwave-safe bowl, add chocolate and butter. Heat for 60 seconds to melt chocolate. Stir until it has melted completely.

2. Mix in 2 tablespoons of peanut butter, heavy cream, and sweetener into melted chocolate.

3. With muffin cups, line a mini muffin tin.

4. Spoon half of the melted chocolate mixture into the cups.

5. Spoon the remaining 2 tablespoons of peanut butter on top of the chocolate in the center of each cup.

6. Pour the remaining chocolate mixture over peanut butter.

7. Freeze for half an hour or until firm.

Flourless Chocolate Cookies

Calories 105 – *Fat* 8g – *Carbs* 3g – *Sugar* 2g – *Protein* 5g

Servings: 12

Ingredients:

- ¼ cup chocolate chips
- 2 tbsp. chocolate protein powder
- 1 egg
- 1 cup almond flour
- 1 cup seed butter of choice

Directions:

1. Preheat oven to 350 degrees. With parchment paper, line a baking tray.

2. Combine all ingredients in a stand mixer, mix it until fully combined.

3. With your hands, form the dough into small golf-sized balls. Place balls on a lined tray and with your palm, press down gently in the center.

4. Bake for 10 to 12 minutes until the edges have browned.

5. Take the cookies out of the oven and let it cool on a tray for 20 minutes before transferring it on a wire rack, allowing it to cool completely.

Dark Chocolate Nut Clusters

Calories 54– Fat 5g – Carbs 3g – Sugar 2g – Protein 1g

Servings: 20

Ingredients:

- 1 package of dark chocolate melting wafers
- 20 walnuts, halves
- 20 pecan, halves
- 20 almonds
- Sea salt

Directions:

1. In a microwavable bowl, add your chocolate wafers. Microwave for 30 seconds until it has completely melted.

2. Dip the walnuts into the melted chocolate with the help of a fork, shaking off the excess. Transfer covered walnuts onto a piece of wax paper. Repeat with pecans, placing it on top of the walnuts, and then with almonds, placing it on top of the cluster to finish off the chocolate stacks.

3. Add a pinch of sea salt to each cluster and allow everything to set before indulging.

Strawberry Cheesecake Fat Bombs

Calories 37 – *Fat* 8g – *Carbs* 2g – *Sugar* 3g – *Protein* 1g

Servings: 12

Ingredients:

- 1 tbsp. vanilla extract
- 10 to 15 drops liquid stevia
- ¼ cup softened butter
- ¾ cup softened cream cheese
- ½ cup frozen or fresh strawberries

Directions:

1. In a bowl, place the butter and cream cheese. Let it sit for 30 to 60 minutes until soft.

2. Wash strawberries and remove the green portions. Mash with a fork until smooth.

3. Add stevia and vanilla to softened cream cheese mixture and combine well.

4. When strawberries have reached room temperature, add to cream cheese mixture, folding well to incorporate.

5. With a hand mixer, mix until combined.

6. Spoon mixture into molds and freeze for two hours

7. Unmold fat bombs and enjoy!

Coconut Crack Bars

Calories 108 – Fat 11g – Carbs 2g – Sugar 2g – Protein 2g

Servings: *20*

Ingredients:

- ¼ cup monk fruit
- 1 cup melted coconut oil
- 3 cup shredded unsweetened coconut flakes

Directions:

1. With parchment paper, line a 8x10 pan.

2. Stir melted coconut oil to shredded unsweetened coconut. Then add monk fruit, keep stirring until the batter thickens.

3. Pour the batter into a lined pan.

4. Wet your hands slightly and press the mixture firmly into pan.

5. Freeze until it's firm. Cut up the bars and enjoy to your heart's content!

Chocolate Chip Oatmeal Cookies

Calories 99– *Fat* 3g – *Carbs* 19g – *Sugar* 8g – *Protein* 2g

Servings: 8

Ingredients:

- ¼ cup chocolate chips
- 1 cup uncooked oats
- 2 mashed ripe bananas

Directions:

1. Preheat your oven to 350 degrees Fahrenheit. Grease a cookie sheet with cooking spray.

2. Combine oats and mashed bananas together.

3. Fold in chocolate chips and drop tablespoons of dough onto the prepared sheet.

4. Bake for 15 minutes.

Crust-Less Cheesecake

Calories 99– *Fat* 3g – *Carbs* 19g – *Sugar* 8g – *Protein* 2g

Servings: 8

Ingredients:

- Big handful of fresh strawberries
- 2 room-temp eggs
- 1 tsp. vanilla extract
- 2/3 cup sugar substitute of your choice
- 2 8-ounce blocks of full-fat cream cheese

Directions:

1. Grease a spring form pan.

2. Blend cream cheese with a hand mixer until smooth.

3. Mix vanilla and sugar substitute with cream cheese until it has blended well together.

4. Add eggs, mixing in one at a time. Be careful to not over mix.

5. Pour batter into the pan. Cover sides and bottom with foil so that water doesn't leak into the pan.

6. Put the rack into the bottom of the instant pot.

7. Add just enough water to cover the bottom.

8. Place the springform pan into the instant pot.

9. Cook on MANUAL and HIGH for 20 minutes.

Strawberries Romanoff

Calories 79– *Fat* 3g – *Carbs* 15g – *Sugar* 12g –
Protein 1g

Servings: 5

Ingredients:

- 2 tbsp. brown sugar
- 4-ounces sour cream
- 16-ounces strawberries

Directions:

1. Mix the brown sugar and sour cream together.

2. Wash and cut up the strawberries.

3. In serving glasses, add five strawberries and drizzle fruit with 2 tbsp. of cream sauce.

4. Enjoy this easy dessert!

Pumpkin Purée

Calories 94– *Fat* 11g – *Carbs* 13g – *Sugar* 8g – *Protein* 4g

Servings: *Varies*

Ingredients:

- 2-pound sugar pumpkin

Directions:

1. Add ½ cup of water to your instant pot.

2. Place the pumpkin on a rack inside your instant pot. Set it to cook on high pressure for 13 to 15 minutes.

3. Perform a quick release of pressure and set it aside to cool.

4. Scoop flesh from the pumpkin and add to the blender. Purée until smooth.

Chapter 12:
Dressings and Sauces

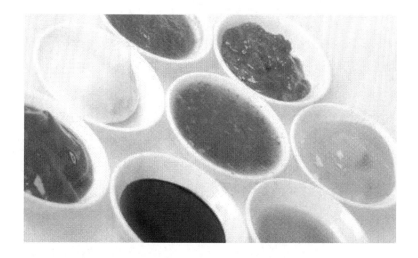

Pickled Mayo Dressing

Calories 115 – *Fat* 10g – *Carbs* 1g – *Sugar* 1g – *Protein* 2g

Servings: 3-4

Ingredients:

- ¼ - ½ tsp. sea salt
- 3 tbsp. pickle juice
- 2 tbsp. Dijon mustard
- ½ cup avocado oil mayo

Directions:

1. Add all dressing ingredients to a blender, along with a pinch of pepper.

2. Blend until smooth.

Raspberry Vinaigrette

Calories 84 – Fat 9g – Carbs 0.5g – Sugar 1g – Protein 0.5g

Servings: 2-4

Ingredients:

- ½ cup golden raspberries
- 35 drops of liquid stevia
- ½ cup extra virgin olive oil
- ½ cup white wine vinegar

Directions:

1. Mix liquid stevia, olive oil, and vinegar together in a vessel that an immersion blender can fit into.

2. Add raspberries and blend with your immersion blender.

3. Strain discarded seeds from the vinaigrette.

4. Enjoy it with your favorite salads!

Cranberry Pear Sauce

Calories 61– *Fat* 0g – *Carbs* 11g – *Sugar* 13g – *Protein* 0g

Servings: 13

Ingredients:

- 1 cup water
- ½ cup honey
- 2 ripe pears
- 12-ounces cranberries

Directions:

1. Peel and core pears. Then cut them into small cubes.

2. Add all the ingredients to a saucepan and bring the mixture to a boil.

3. Once it boils, decrease heat and let it simmer for 15 minutes until the cranberries start to burst and the sauce thickens.

4. Take it off the heat and let it cool.

5. Allow it to chill in the fridge or keep at room temperature, your choice.

Keto`Garlic Alfredo Sauce

Calories 89– Fat 5g – Carbs 2g – Sugar 4g – Protein 0g

Servings: 4

Ingredients:

- 1 tsp. garlic powder
- ¼ tsp. salt
- 1 cup shredded parmesan cheese
- 1 cup heavy whipping cream
- ½ cup butter

Directions:

1. Slowly melt the butter over low heat.

2. Mix in salt, garlic powder, and whipping cream with butter. Increase heat.

3. Add parmesan cheese, keep stirring until it melts.

4. Serve over whole wheat noodles!

Keto Buffalo Sauce

Calories 61– *Fat* 0g – *Carbs* 11g – *Sugar* 13g – *Protein* 0g

Servings: 13

Ingredients:

- ½ tsp. garlic powder
- 1 tsp. apple cider vinegar
- 1 tbsp. coconut aminos
- 2 ½ tbsp. ghee
- ½ cup red hot sauce

Directions:

1. Add all the ingredients to a pan over medium heat. When ghee melts, whisk well to combine.

2. Pour any sauce you do not plan to use right away inside a glass jar with lid. It can be chilled in a fridge for up to 2 weeks.

Chapter 13:
My Favorite Ketogenic Ingredients

Man, oh man, is there a lot to like about the ketogenic diet or what? Before you get yourself pumped up to go to the grocery store with your keto-inspired list, I want to discuss some of my favorite ketogenic diet ingredients that I always have a fresh stock of in the kitchen (and you should too!).

Seafood

Shellfish and fish are very keto-friendly. However, keep in mind that the carb content in fish can vary, unlike other carb sources. For example, most crabs and all shrimps have no carbs, while other shellfish do. All fish is loaded with essential vitamins, minerals, and omega-3s.

Low-carb veggies

Vegetables that are low in starch content are high in nutrients and low in carbs, which makes them a staple for keto diet. They are also a great source of vitamin C and fiber. These also make for awesome substitutes for foods that have a higher carb count. The more cruciferous the vegetable, the better!

Cheese

Cheese is not only delicious but nutritious! There are literally hundreds of kinds of cheeses, with most of them being high in fat and low in carbs. It also contains conjugated linoleic acid, which has been proven to help with weight loss.

Avocados

High in vitamins and minerals, avocados are one of those ingredients that can make your transition to the keto diet much easier. They also help improve your triglyceride and cholesterol levels.

Meat and poultry

These are staples on the keto diet and are loaded with B vitamins and essential minerals, such as zinc and potassium. This staple is rich in proteins, giving you the energy you need to do your best.

Eggs

Eggs are not only only versatile but also healthy. An egg has less than a gram of carbs and is made up of six grams of protein, which makes it an ideal keto staple.

Coconut oil

Coconut oil contains several unique properties that makes it a well-suited component for the keto diet. This oil is an essential ingredient in increasing ketone levels and helps sustain sufficient levels of ketosis.

Cottage cheese and plain Greek yogurt

These two dairy products are high in protein and very healthy. They help keep your stomach satisfied for longer periods of time and reduce overall appetite. Plus, either of them on their own makes very tasty snacks. I like to combine them with cinnamon and chopped nuts!

Olive oil

This oil is impressive because of its many heart benefits. It's loaded with many antioxidants that further protects this vital organ and decreases inflammation throughout the body.

Nuts and seeds

Seeds and nut are high in healthy fats and are extremely tasty. Frequently consuming them can lead to a decrease in heart disease and depression. High in fiber, they promote healthy aging as well, keeping you satiated between meals.

Berries

While majority of fruits have a high carb content, berries are a tasty exception. These itty-bitty fruits are packed with antioxidants and are known to reduce inflammation and protect your body from many diseases.

Cream and butter

Despite popular belief, both cream and butter are considered healthy fats for keto and are foundational staples on this diet. They contribute to heart health and promote healthy weight loss.

Shirataki noodles

Many people forget about these delicious guys. Since they are mainly just water, it allows food to move slower through your digestive tract which results in reduced appetite and better control over blood sugars.

Olives

Olives provide many of the same benefits of their cousin, olive oil, just in solid form. They contain anti-inflammatory properties and decrease blood pressure. They are also known to decrease bone loss.

Unsweetened tea and coffee

Tea and coffee are extremely healthy when you forego all those extra, carb-filled ingredients that we can't seem to resist. Caffeine increases your metabolism which helps to enhance mood and performance. It also drastically lowers the development of diabetes. If you must add cream to your cup of Joe, that is fine, but never opt for light coffees or tea lattes. These are loaded with non-fat milk and are high on carbs.

Cocoa powder and dark chocolate

For all those chocolate lovers out there, you will be glad to hear these two items are on the keto list of delicious staples. Cocoa is actually a superfood since it provides high levels of antioxidants. Dark chocolate contains flavanols that help to reduce the development of heart disease and lowers blood pressure. Opt for 70% cocoa or higher when buying dark chocolate.

Conclusion

I want to congratulate you for making it to the end of the *5 Ingredients Ketosis Diet Plans*.

As you have read, it is quite possible to engage in a healthier lifestyle without the stress of shopping for endless ingredients and slaving away in your kitchen. That is why many of the recipes you have read comprised of cooking methods that involve you swiching on a button and simply walking away. So, how much easier can it get?

This is the cookbook that will take over all your other recipe books that are lined up in your kitchen countertops. Whether you are planning to fulfill your New Year's resolution of losing some weight, or if you just want to be healthier, look better and feel your best, these recipes are the building blocks to achieving your health and fitness goals!

I encourage you to begin utilizing the recipes in this book in your everyday life. You will soon discover that being healthier doesn't mean having to sacrifice your taste buds!

If you found this cookbook to be of value in any way, please take a moment to leave us a review on Amazon. It will be much appreciated!

Made in the USA
San Bernardino, CA
17 February 2020